ideals ®
CHRISTMAS

Come, sing a hale Heigh-ho
For the Christmas long ago! —
When the old log cabin homed us
From the night of blinding snow,

Where the rarest joy held reign,
And the chimney roared amain,
With the firelight like a beacon
Through the frosty windowpane.

James Whitcomb Riley

ISBN 0-8249-1031-1 350

Publisher, Patricia A. Pingry
Editor/Ideals, Kathleen S. Pohl
Managing Editor, Marybeth Owens
Art Director, William Scholz
Production Manager, Mark Brunner
Photographic Editor, Gerald Koser
Manuscript Editor, Naomi Galbreath
Research Editor, Linda Robinson

IDEALS—Vol. 41, No. 8 November MCMLXXXIV IDEALS (ISSN 0019-137X) is published eight times a year,
February, March, April, June, August, September, November, December
by IDEALS PUBLISHING CORPORATION, 11315 Watertown Plank Road, Milwaukee, Wis. 53226
Second class postage paid at Milwaukee, Wisconsin and additional mailing offices.
Copyright © MCMLXXXIV by IDEALS PUBLISHING CORPORATION.
POSTMASTER: Send address changes to Ideals, Post Office Box 2100, Milwaukee, Wis. 53201
All rights reserved. Title IDEALS registered U.S. Patent Office.
Published simultaneously in Canada.

ONE YEAR SUBSCRIPTION—eight consecutive issues as published—$15.95
TWO YEAR SUBSCRIPTION—sixteen consecutive issues as published—$27.95
SINGLE ISSUE—$3.50
Outside U.S.A., add $4.00 per subscription year for postage and handling

*Front and
back covers
Gerald Koser*

A Christmas Wish

More than a Merry Christmas
I wish you this year,
More than a Happy Christmas
With your loved ones dear,
More than the precious hours
With friends who are true,
More than the gifts you treasure
That others give you —
I wish for you the blessing
Of that Christmas day
When angels sang the story
And stars marked the way.
I wish you joy unending
With much love and cheer —
I wish you peace on Christmas
And through all the year.

Grace Mathews Walker

Photo opposite
CHRISTMAS MAIL
Fred Sieb

December

I like days
with a snow-white collar,
and nights when the moon
is a silver dollar,
and hills are filled
with eiderdown stuffing
and your breath makes smoke
like an engine puffing.

I like days
when feathers are snowing,
and all the eaves
have petticoats showing,
and the air is cold,
and the wires are humming,
but you feel all warm . . .
with Christmas coming!

Aileen Fisher

The Snowflake

Before I melt,
Come, look at me!
This lovely icy filigree!
Of a great forest
In one night
I make a wilderness
Of white:
By skyey cold
Of crystals made,
All softly, on
Your finger laid,
I pause, that you
My beauty see:
Breathe, and I vanish
Instantly.

Walter de la Mare

Velvet Shoes

Let us walk in the white snow
    In a soundless space;
With footsteps quiet and slow,
    At a tranquil pace,
    Under veils of white lace.

I shall go shod in silk,
    And you in wool,
White as a white cow's milk,
    More beautiful
    Than the breast of a gull.

We shall walk through the still town
    In a windless peace;
We shall step upon white down,
    Upon silver fleece,
    Upon softer than these.

We shall walk in velvet shoes:
    Wherever we go
Silence will fall like dews
    On white silence below.
    We shall walk in the snow.

Elinor Wylie

Photo opposite
WOODLAND SNOW
Josef Muench

The Last Minute Rush

We begin to think of Christmas
Around Thanksgiving Day
And make our lists and purchase cards
But it still seems far away.
Quite leisurely, we look for gifts
Each time we're in a store
To be sure last minute shopping
Shan't besiege us as before.

Then suddenly we realize
It's but two short weeks away,
And we join the crowds out shopping
With no time left to delay.
We address cards and mail them
While regretting so much haste,
Wrap packages to hide or mail —
Not a moment can we waste.

We put candles in the windows,
Hang the sprig of mistletoe;
The holly wreath goes on the door
With its perky scarlet bow.
Then the turkey must be ordered
And the goodies that we buy.
Cranberry sauce should soon be made,
And the mince and pumpkin pie.

There are programs needing costumes
And some treats for parties too,
And driving kids to these affairs
Is a task we'll have to do.
That same last minute rush again —
But we somehow get it done,
And after all it's Christmastime,
And the rush is rather fun!

Harriet Whipple

To a Christmas Tree

O balsam tree, that lately held
The stars like nesting birds among
Your emerald branches, listen now
To children's voices sweet with song!

You talker with the wind, and friend
Of fox and fawn and silver mouse,
Bearing your tinsel and your gifts,
Glow softly now within this house,

Bringing your fragrance to our hearts,
Assuring us that wars will cease.
For a Child's bright birthday shine with faith,
O tree of loveliness and peace!

Frances Frost

From THE LITTLE WHISTLER by Frances Frost, copyright, 1949 by McGraw-Hill Book
Company, Inc. Reprinted by permission.

Painting opposite
CHRISTMAS FAMILY
Richard Hook

Home for Christmas

This is meeting time again. Home is the magnet. The winter land roars and hums with the eager speed of return journeys. The dark is noisy and bright with late-night arrivals — doors thrown open, running shadows on snow, open arms, kisses, voices and laughter, laughter at everything and nothing. Inarticulate, giddying and confused are those original minutes of being back again. The very familiarity of everything acts like shock. Contentment has to be drawn in slowly, steadyingly, in deep breaths — there is so much of it. We rely on home not to change, and it does not, wherefore we give thanks. Again Christmas: abiding point of return. Set apart by its mystery, mood and magic, the season seems in a way to stand outside time. All that is dear, that is lasting, renews its hold on us: we are home again....

This glow of Christmas, has it not in it also the gold of a harvest? "They shall return with joy, bringing their sheaves with them." To the festival, to each other, we bring in wealth. More to tell, more to under-

HOME FOR CHRISTMAS by Elizabeth Bowen is from THE FAMILY CHRISTMAS BOOK © 1957 by Prentice-Hall Inc. Used by permission of Curtis Brown Ltd, London literary executors of the late Elizabeth Bowen.

Stan
Ekman

stand, more to share. Each we have garnered in yet another year; to be glad, to celebrate to the full, we are come together. How akin we are to each other, how speechlessly dear and one in the fundamentals of being; Christmas shows us. No other time grants us, quite, this vision — round the tree or gathered before the fire we perceive anew, with joy, one another's faces. And each time faces come to mean more.

Is it not one of the mysteries of life that life should, after all, be so simple? Yes, as simple as Christmas, simple as this. Journeys through the dark to a lighted door, arms open. Laughter-smothered kisses, kiss-smothered laughter. And blessedness in the heart of it all. Here are the verities, all made gay with tinsel! Dear, silly Christmas-card saying and cracker mottoes — let them speak! Or, since still we cannot speak, let us sing! Dearer than memory, brighter than expectation is the ever returning *now* of Christmas. Why else, each time we greet its return, should happiness ring out in us like a peal of bells?

From *Home for Christmas* by Elizabeth Bowen

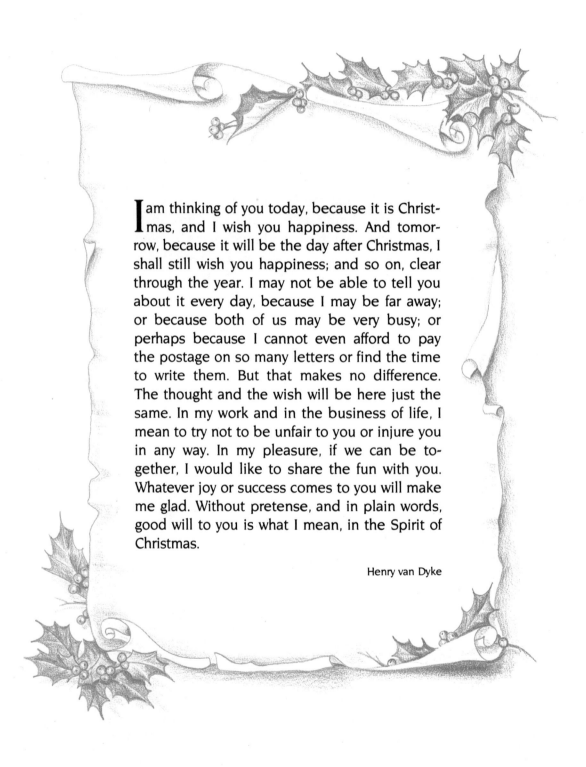

I am thinking of you today, because it is Christmas, and I wish you happiness. And tomorrow, because it will be the day after Christmas, I shall still wish you happiness; and so on, clear through the year. I may not be able to tell you about it every day, because I may be far away; or because both of us may be very busy; or perhaps because I cannot even afford to pay the postage on so many letters or find the time to write them. But that makes no difference. The thought and the wish will be here just the same. In my work and in the business of life, I mean to try not to be unfair to you or injure you in any way. In my pleasure, if we can be together, I would like to share the fun with you. Whatever joy or success comes to you will make me glad. Without pretense, and in plain words, good will to you is what I mean, in the Spirit of Christmas.

Henry van Dyke

Thoughts
on Christmas

I have always thought of Christmas time, when it has come round... as a good time: a kind, forgiving, charitable, pleasant time: the only time I know of, in the long calendar of the year, when men and women seem by one consent to open their shut-up hearts freely, and to think of people below them as if they really were fellow passengers to the grave, and not another race of creatures bound on other journeys. And therefore... though it has never put a scrap of gold or silver in my pocket, I believe that it *has* done me good, and *will* do me good; and I say, God bless it!

Charles Dickens

A Child's Christmas in Wales

One Christmas was so much like another, in those years around the sea-town corner now and out of all sound except the distant speaking of the voices I sometimes hear a moment before sleep, that I can never remember whether it snowed for six days and six nights when I was twelve or whether it snowed for twelve days and twelve nights when I was six....

Years and years and years ago, when I was a boy, when there were wolves in Wales, and birds the color of red-flannel petticoats whisked past the harp-shaped hills, when we sang and wallowed all night and day in caves that smelt like Sunday afternoons in damp front farmhouse parlors, and we chased, with the jawbones of deacons, the English and the bears, before the motor car, before the wheel, before the duchess-faced horse when we rode the daft and happy hills bareback, it snowed and it snowed. But here a small boy says: "It snowed last year, too. I made a snowman and my brother knocked it down and I knocked my brother down and then we had tea."

"But that was not the same snow," I say. "Our snow was not only shaken from whitewash buckets down the sky, it came shawling out of the ground and swam and drifted out of the arms and hands and bodies of the trees; snow grew overnight on the roofs of the houses like a pure and grandfather moss, minutely white-ivied the walls and settled on the postman, opening the gate, like a dumb, numb thunderstorm of white, torn Christmas cards."

"Were there postmen then, too?"

"With sprinkling eyes and wind-cherried noses, on spread, frozen feet they crunched up to the doors and mittened on them manfully. But all that the children could hear was a ringing of bells."

"You mean that the postman went rat-a-tat-tat and the doors rang?"

"I mean that the bells that the children could hear were inside them."

"I only hear thunder sometimes, never bells."

"There were church bells, too."

"Inside them?"

"No, no, no, in the bat-black, snow-white belfries, tugged by bishops and storks. And they rang their tidings over the bandaged town, over the frozen foam of the powder and ice-cream hills, over the crackling sea. It seemed that all the churches boomed for joy under my window; and the weathercocks crew for Christmas, on our fence...."

For dinner we had turkey and blazing pudding, and after dinner the Uncles sat in front of the fire, loosened all buttons, put their large moist hands over their watch chains, groaned a little and slept. Mothers, aunts and sisters scuttled to and fro, bearing tureens....

I would blow up balloons to see how big they would blow up to; and, when they burst, which they all did, the Uncles jumped and rumbled. In the rich and heavy afternoon, the Uncles breathing like dolphins and the snow descending, I would sit among festoons and Chinese lanterns and nibble dates and try to make a model man-o'-war, following the Instructions for Little Engineers, and produce what might be mistaken for a sea-going tramcar. Or I would go out, my bright new boots squeaking, into the white world, on to the seaward hill, to call on Jim and Dan and Jack and to pad through the still streets, leaving huge deep footprints on the hidden pavements....

Always on Christmas night there was music. An uncle played the fiddle, a cousin sang "Cherry Ripe," and another uncle sang "Drake's Drum." It was very warm in the little house....

Looking through my bedroom window, out into the moonlight and the unending smoke-colored snow, I could see the lights in the windows of all the other houses on our hill and hear the music rising from them up the long, steadily falling night. I turned the gas down, I got into bed. I said some words to the close and holy darkness, and then I slept.

Dylan Thomas

The Gingerbread House

Deep in the forest where all dreams come true
Is a gingerbread house just waiting for you.
Its roof is a mixture of sugar and spice
And the chimney is made of everything nice.

Bright colored bonbons grow round the front door,
And chocolate cookies are laid for the floor.
Its walls made of cookies are cheerful and gay,
And they make this house seem like a nice place to stay.

The house is surrounded by green sugar trees,
And you may eat just as much as you please...
Deep in the forest where all dreams come true
Is a gingerbread house just waiting for you!

Patricia Mongeau

Gingerbread House

(To construct Gingerbread House pictured on previous page, follow recipes and instructions below and use pattern pieces provided on opposite page.)

Gingerbread Dough

5 cups shortening
5 cups brown sugar, packed
5 tablespoons cinnamon
6 tablespoons ginger
10 eggs
5 cups dark corn syrup
8 teaspoons baking soda
28 cups flour

Cream shortening, sugar, and spices in a large mixing bowl. Beat in eggs. Add corn syrup; blend well. Mix baking soda and flour together in separate bowl. Add ½ of the flour mixture to creamed ingredients; beat well. Stir in remaining flour mixture; beat until smooth. Wrap airtight. Chill at least 5 hours or overnight. Makes enough dough for house, trees, reindeer, and fence in photo.

Decorator Icing

4 pounds confectioners' sugar
12 egg whites
2 teaspoons cream of tartar

In a large mixing bowl, beat all ingredients together for about 10 minutes or until stiff peaks form. Cover with damp towel; take out only as needed, as this frosting hardens quickly. Note: Icing may be stored for several days in refrigerator. Beat again before using.

Christmas Wreath Candy

⅓ cup butter or margarine
20 marshmallows
  Green food coloring
2¼ cups cornflakes

Prepare this candy just before you plan to use it, as it hardens quickly. In microwave or top of double boiler, melt butter and marshmallows. Add food coloring as desired. Remove from heat. Add cornflakes and stir until well coated.

To cut out house: Enlarge pattern pieces to size, drawing on paper or thin cardboard. Cut out pattern. On lightly greased, *inverted* cookie sheet, roll out dough to ³/₁₆" thickness. Dust pattern pieces with flour. Place patterns on dough. Cut through dough with sharp knife. Without moving cut-out pieces, remove patterns and excess dough. Bake in place on *inverted* cookie sheet at 375° F. until lightly browned. Check cookie edges once during baking, straightening edges with a knife, if necessary. When dough is baked and still warm, loosen pieces with spatula. Do not remove from cookie sheets until completely cool. Use same dough and same procedure to make trees, reindeer, and fence, rolling dough somewhat thinner for smaller pieces. Cut tree cookies using pattern pictured. Shape reindeer using cookie cutters. For fence, cut strips of dough in varying lengths. Let baked dough sit 5-6 hours before assembling house.

To assemble house: Use pastry bag with number 4 or 5 tip throughout assembly process. Mortar house with decorator icing, beginning with sides, front and back of house. Wherever seams meet, mortar with icing and press together gently. Prop pieces up with cans until icing sets. Wait overnight before putting on roof. Then thickly mortar with icing where front and back and side pieces meet roof. Press pieces together carefully. Mortar along seam at peak of roof. Assemble chimney pieces and mortar to roof. Let set 1 to 2 hours before decorating.

To decorate house: Using same decorator icing and pastry bag, ice 12 vanilla wafers and dust with red sprinkles. Secure wafers with decorator icing, as pictured. Loop shingles of icing on roof. Thickly squiggle icing unevenly on edges of roof to simulate snow. Ice life savers to side of house. Line silver beads along roof top.

Decorate front of house with jelly rings, life savers, gumdrops, and red hots as pictured. Outline door with icing; attach gumdrop door knob; set aside.

With Christmas Wreath Candy, form wreath around door. Accent with red candy or icing to resemble holly. Mortar or set door in place, leaving slightly ajar.

Outline path with decorator icing and peppermint candy. Mortar gingerbread fence pieces together; place where desired. Sprinkle trees and reindeer lightly with sifted confectioners' sugar. Sprinkle confectioners' sugar around house to simulate snow. Fluff cotton to simulate chimney smoke.

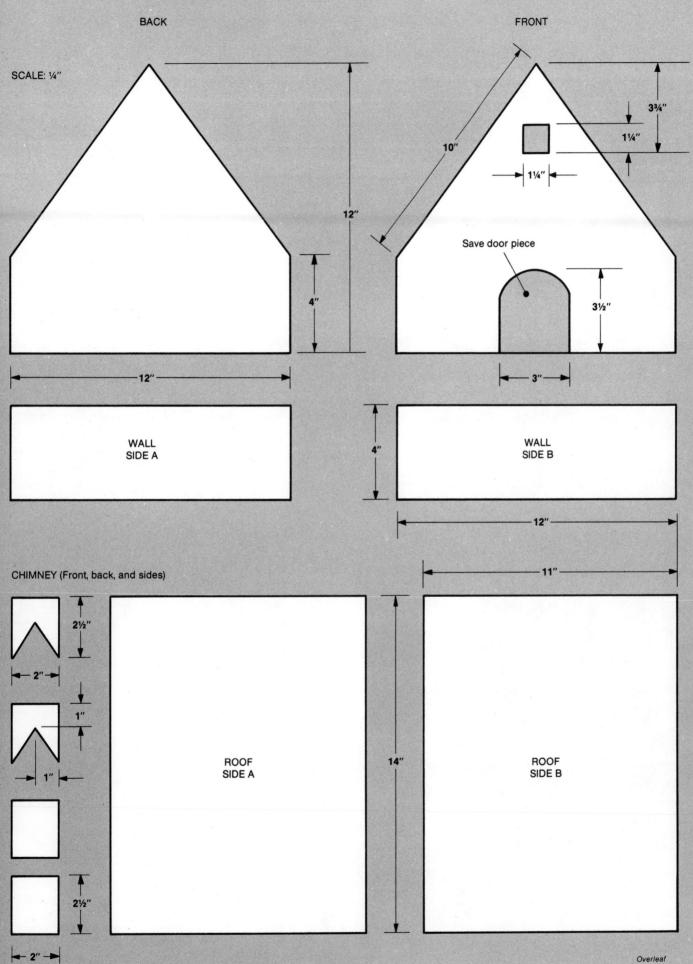

BACK

FRONT

SCALE: ¼"

12"

4"

12"

10"

3¾"

1¼"

1¼"

Save door piece

3½"

3"

WALL
SIDE A

WALL
SIDE B

4"

12"

11"

CHIMNEY (Front, back, and sides)

2½"

2"

1"

1"

2½"

2"

ROOF
SIDE A

ROOF
SIDE B

14"

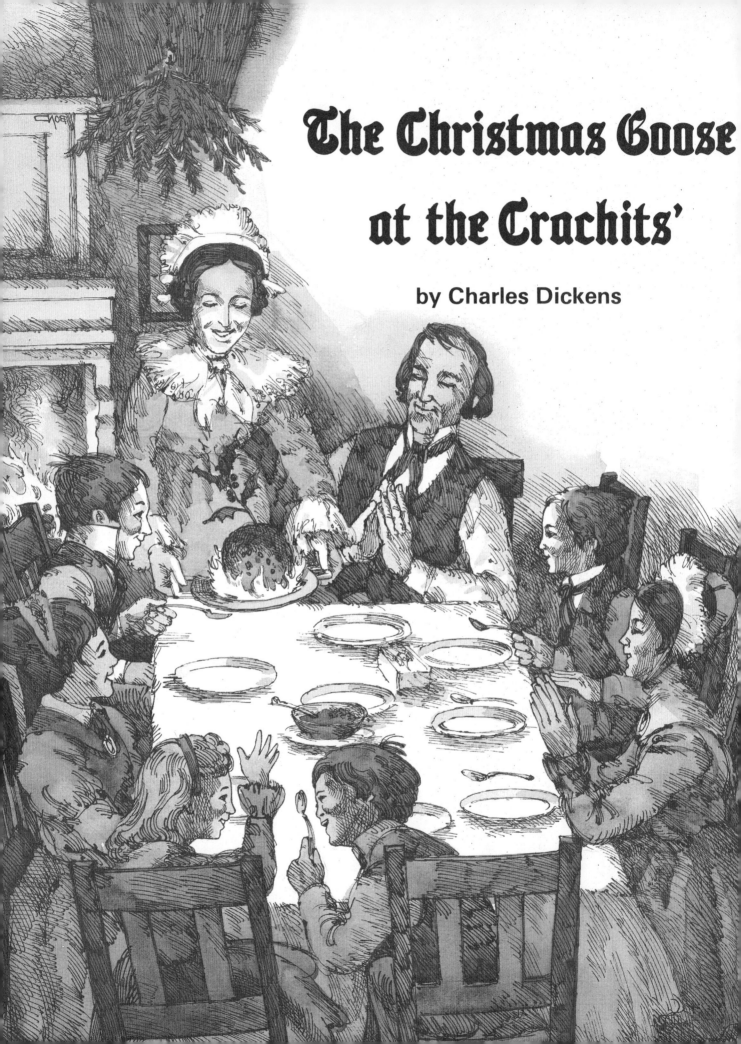

The Christmas Goose at the Crachits'

by Charles Dickens

And gently, then, they set me down,
All worshipping that holy town,
And gently, then, they bade me raise
My head to worship and to praise.

And gently, then, the Christ smiled down.
Ah, there was glory in that town!
It was as if the world were free
And glistening with purity.

And in that vault of crystal blue,
It was as if the world were new,
And myriad angels, file on file,
Gloried in the Christ-Child's smile.

It was so beautiful to see
Such glory, for a child like me,
So beautiful, it does not seem
It could have been a Christmas dream.

John Farrar

Tradition Time

So much of the joy of Christmas
   Is the sameness of it all —
Always the wreath upon the door,
   The festoons in the hall;
The mistletoe hung overhead,
   The squeals at getting captured;
The sparkling tree that holds its viewers
   Silently enraptured.

The same beloved ornaments,
   The candles and the bells;
The same old Christmas stories
   That Grandpa always tells.
The same old battered angel
   Once again adds to the joy —
It's stood atop the tree each year
   Since Grandpa was a boy.

The merry family gatherings —
   The old, the very young;
The strangely lovely way they
   Harmonize in carols sung.
For Christmas is tradition time —
   Traditions that recall
The precious memories down the years,
   The sameness of them all.

Helen Lowrie Marshall

From STARLIGHT AND CANDLEGLOW by Helen Lowrie Marshall. Reprinted by permission of John Stanley Marshall.

The Holly and the Ivy

The Holly and the Ivy,
   When they are both full grown
Of all the trees are in the wood,
   The Holly bears the crown.

O the rising of the sun,
   And the running of the deer,
The playing of the merry organ,
   Sweet singing in the choir.

The Holly bears a blossom
   As white as any flower;
And Mary bore sweet Jesus Christ
   To be our sweet Savior.

The Holly bears a berry
   As red as any blood;
And Mary bore sweet Jesus Christ
   To do poor sinners good.

The Holly bears a prickle
   As sharp as any thorn;
And Mary bore sweet Jesus Christ
   On Christmas in the morn.

The Holly bears a bark
   As bitter as any gall;
And Mary bore sweet Jesus Christ
   For to redeem us all.

The Holly and the Ivy
   Now both are full well grown:
Of all the trees are in the wood
   The Holly bears the crown.

Fifteenth-century English carol

The Christmas Holly

The holly! the holly! oh, twine it with bay —
    Come give the holly a song;
For it helps to drive stern winter away,
    With his garment so sombre and long;

It peeps through the trees with its berries of red
    And its leaves of burnished green,
When the flowers and fruits have long been dead,
    And not even the daisy is seen.
Then sing to the holly, the Christmas holly,
    That hangs over peasant and king;
While we laugh and carouse 'neath its glittering boughs,
    To the Christmas holly we'll sing.

The gale may whistle, the frost may come
    To fetter the gurgling rill;
The woods may be bare, and warblers dumb,
    But holly is beautiful still.
In the revel and light of princely halls
    The bright holly branch is found;
And its shadow falls on the lowliest walls,
    While the brimming horn goes round.

The ivy lives long, but its home must be
    Where graves and ruins are spread;
There's beauty about the cypress tree,
    But it flourishes near the dead;
The laurel the warrior's brow may wreathe,
    But it tells of tears and blood;
I sing the holly, and who can breathe
    Aught of that that is not good?
Then sing to the holly, the Christmas holly,
    That hangs over peasant and king;
While we laugh and carouse 'neath its glittering boughs,
    To the Christmas holly we'll sing.

Eliza Cook

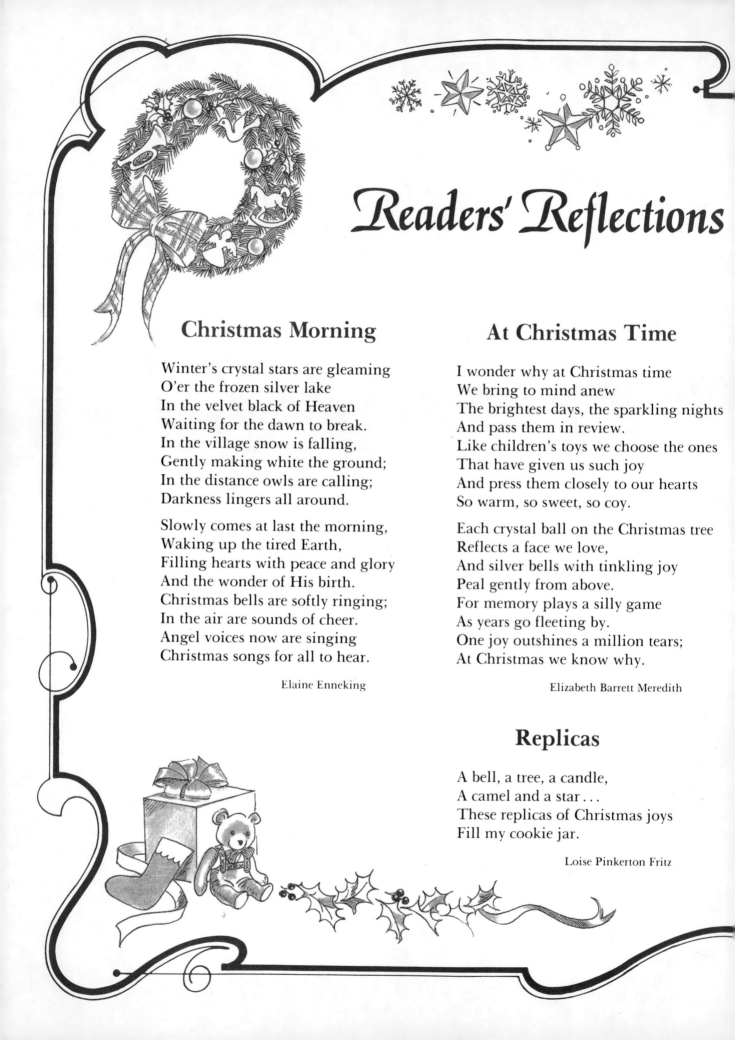

Readers' Reflections

Christmas Morning

Winter's crystal stars are gleaming
O'er the frozen silver lake
In the velvet black of Heaven
Waiting for the dawn to break.
In the village snow is falling,
Gently making white the ground;
In the distance owls are calling;
Darkness lingers all around.

Slowly comes at last the morning,
Waking up the tired Earth,
Filling hearts with peace and glory
And the wonder of His birth.
Christmas bells are softly ringing;
In the air are sounds of cheer.
Angel voices now are singing
Christmas songs for all to hear.

Elaine Enneking

At Christmas Time

I wonder why at Christmas time
We bring to mind anew
The brightest days, the sparkling nights
And pass them in review.
Like children's toys we choose the ones
That have given us such joy
And press them closely to our hearts
So warm, so sweet, so coy.

Each crystal ball on the Christmas tree
Reflects a face we love,
And silver bells with tinkling joy
Peal gently from above.
For memory plays a silly game
As years go fleeting by.
One joy outshines a million tears;
At Christmas we know why.

Elizabeth Barrett Meredith

Replicas

A bell, a tree, a candle,
A camel and a star...
These replicas of Christmas joys
Fill my cookie jar.

Loise Pinkerton Fritz

Editor's Note: Readers are invited to submit poetry, short anecdotes, and humorous reflections on life for possible publication in future *Ideals* issues. Writers will receive $10 for each published submission. Send material to "Readers' Reflections," P.O. Box 1101, Milwaukee, Wisconsin 53201.

Junior's Train

On Christmas morning Junior is
A wistful little boy,
For Daddy claims the 'lectric train
As were it his own toy.
He tests the engine and caboose.
He tests the signals, too,
And lays out every piece of track —
No wonder Junior's blue.

Dad finds that the instructions are
A little bit amiss,
And for that reason Christmas morn
Is anything but bliss.
But when at last it's football time,
And when the game's begun,
Daddy drops the doggone train —
And Junior makes it run.

Minnie Klemme

Christmas through the Year

A little bit of Christmas lives
Within the heart each day,
When you do a kindly deed,
Give a word of cheer away.
Why should we save our kindnesses
For just one special time —
The world needs love and caring
When Christmas bells don't chime!

Reach out a hand to help someone;
Cheer some heart today.
The gifts that mean the most
Aren't those for which we pay.
Though tinseled scenes have faded
That mark the yuletide cheer,
Christmas living in the heart
Grows brighter through the year!

Kay Hoffman

Christmas

Christmas is a time of magic:
Lighted trees and glowing fires,
Spicy smells of Christmas baking,
Carol music from church choirs.

Bess Meredith

A Christmas Meditation

So Christmas takes its place as part of the unchanging pattern. The old ways change, but the spirit does not change. It does not matter what the gift is, because the giving and not the gift is the verity — the giving and the receiving. And the giving and receiving signify and prove that the spirit is not dead. In the humdrum of daily life it might easily be believed by the despondent, harried soul, which sometimes anyone is, that all is selfishness and coldness of heart, that love is lost. Then Christmas comes and in the symbolism of its giving and receiving among those we know and love and the unknown, the poor and lonely in every community, we find our faith renewed because our own hearts are warmed again to life and love.

Yes, we need Christmas. Christians have made Christmas, but in every religion everywhere in the world there are days which mean Christmas, days of renewal of peace and goodwill among men. The ways in which we express the day's meaning differ in time and place but the meaning never changes. The blessed Christmas spirit descends upon us even in this year...And so, God bless us all.

Pearl S. Buck

Photo opposite
HOLIDAY BLOOMS
Gerald Koser

Harriet Whipple

Harriet Whipple was born in Pennsylvania in 1905. She has lived in towns and cities of New York state since the age of four.

At age eleven Mrs. Whipple wrote her first poem. She has been writing poetry ever since.

Many magazines and newspapers have published Mrs. Whipple's poetry. A large reader response has led to pen-pals around the nation, one of whom is Garnett Ann Schultz, another *Ideals* Best-Loved Poet. Their correspondence has continued for seventeen years.

In 1983 Mrs. Whipple's first book of collected poems was published. We all look forward to the second volume, to be published soon.

Christmas Is Coming

We're seeing manger scenes about
And hearing carols once more;
Christmas is coming nearer now,
And Santa is in each store.
They're selling trees of evergreen
To trim with glowing lights.
Counters are laden high with toys
In which each child delights.

There are candles in the windows
And wreathes upon each door
With mistletoe and holly
Just where they were before.
Closets are full of packages
All wrapped and marked with care,
And in many secret places
Gifts are hidden here and there.

Each kitchen's now a busy place
And smells extremely nice
As the cookies, pies, and fruitcakes
Send forth the scents of spice.
There are smiles on all the faces
Of shoppers that we meet,
For there is Christmas spirit
In everyone we greet.

Cards come in with every mail
And Santa socks appear;
Children count remaining days
Till Christmas day is here.
We're hoping for a bit of snow
To make a festive scene,
For Christmas isn't quite as bright
If the outdoor world is green.

Our Christmas Message

May the Christmas Spirit fill your heart
  With love and joy today
To bring you peace and happiness
  In every special way.

May the memories of Christmases
  Glow warmly in your heart
Where the cherished old traditions
  Ever play a vital part.

May the day be extra special
  With the beauty of some snow;
May the sunshine make it sparkle
  And bring a festive glow.

May the candles, bells, and holly,
  The cards and gifts and flowers
Fill the day with cheerfulness
  And lovely happy hours.

May those you love surround you
  To share your Christmas day;
May the blessings of the season
  Come in your life to stay.

That Time Again

Now is the time for greeting cards
  We all enjoy each year
With merry Christmas wishes
  For loved ones far and near.

It's the time for Christmas shopping,
  For buying presents and toys,
For choosing just the perfect thing
  That we know each friend enjoys,

For wrapping up the packages,
  Each topped with a fancy bow,
And hiding them all secretly
  Where only we shall know.

It's the time for decorating
  With holly and mistletoe,
For setting up the Christmas tree
  And the manger scene below.

It's the time for singing carols —
  All the old-time ones we love,
And to hear the Christmas story
  Of the gift from God above.

Christmas Eve

I stood by my window at midnight —
  Tired but happy — and thankful too
That the preparations were finished,
  And I'd done all I'd planned to do.
The tree looked really splendid
  With its colored lights aglow,
And the living room was festive
  With plants and mistletoe.
The children were peacefully sleeping,
  And "Santa Claus" dozed in his chair,
Tired from the many excursions
  To bring down the gifts from up there.
The goodies for feasting were ready;
  The holly wreath hung on the door.
We'd filled the red Christmas stockings
  And piled all the gifts on the floor,

Thankful to grant fondest wishes —
  Anticipating delight,
Happy that loved ones would gather
  To make our Christmas just right.
It was like a Christmas card outside —
  Bright stars and sparkling snow,
With each home all gayly lighted
  To enhance the holiday glow.
I was filled with Christmas spirit
  As I looked on the lovely sight.
Then one star seemed to grow larger,
  And I thought of that long ago night
When a star led kings and shepherds
  To a Babe asleep in the hay.
Let us never fail to remember
  Why we celebrate Christmas Day!

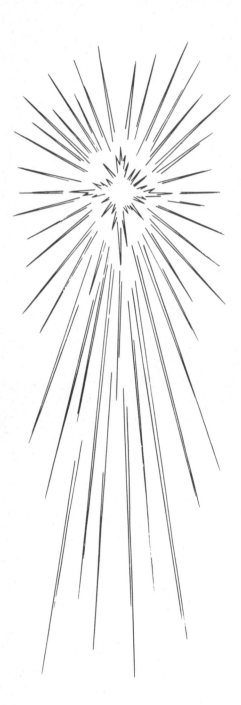

Christmas Everywhere

Everywhere, everywhere, Christmas tonight!
Christmas in lands of the fir-tree and pine,
Christmas in lands of the palm-tree and vine,
Christmas where snow peaks stand solemn and white,
Christmas where corn fields stand sunny and bright.
Christmas where children are hopeful and gay,
Christmas where old men are patient and gray,
Christmas where peace, like a dove in his flight,
Broods o'er brave men in the thick of the fight;

Everywhere, everywhere, Christmas tonight!
For the Christ-Child who comes is the Master of all;
No palace too great, no cottage too small.

Phillips Brooks

'Twas the Bike before Christmas

'Twas the night before Christmas, when all through our house
Not a creature was sleeping, not even my spouse.
The stockings were hung by the chimney with screws.
(If you can't find the nails, what else do you use?)
The children were restless, awake in their beds,
While visions of spanking them danced in our heads.
I worked in my bathrobe. My husband, in jeans,
Had gone down to the den with directions and dreams
To assemble a bike that came in small pieces
With deflated tires and fenders with creases.
Soon down in the den there arose such a clatter,
I sprang from my task to see what was the matter.
Away to my husband I flew like a flash;
He was shuffling through cardboard; his actions were rash.
The bike on the rug by this now flustered Dad
Soon gave me a hint as to why he was mad.
He needed a kickstand. It had to be near.
I shuffled some papers — he saw it appear!
We twisted the screws; we were lively and quick,
And we soon knew assembly would be quite a trick.
Fast as eagles in flight the pieces were found,
And he whistled and shouted for parts all around:
"Now socket! Now pedal! Now tires! Now brakes!
On handles! On kickstand! On horn!...oh...but wait!"
In the top of the toolbox, he fumbled around;
"I need two more screws!" he said with a frown.
And like all good parents determined to please
When they meet with an obstacle late Christmas Eve,
We shouted and yelled some complaints to each other.
There was never more frustrated father and mother!

And then, in a panic, we heard on the stairs
The prancing and hopping of feet . . . 'bout two pairs!
I opened the door and was turning around,
When kids burst from the hall with a leap and a bound.
They were dressed all in flannel, from their necks to their knees,
And their nightgowns were soiled with sugar and cheese!
Excuses poured forth from each pair of lips;
They stood in defiance with hands on their hips.
Their eyes were wide open, and each little child
Jumped when I yelled with a voice hardly mild.
They were frightened but cute, though much bigger than elves,
And we laughed when we saw them, in spite of ourselves.
A wink of the eye and a pat on the head
Soon let them both know they had nothing to dread.
They saw not a thing but went straight to their beds,
And we finished the bike and put bows on the sleds.
Then wheeling the bike by the tree (out of sight),
My hubby announced we should call it a night.
He sprang to his bed, to the clock gave a whistle,
As the time had flown by like a large Titan missile.
But I heard him exclaim as he turned out the light,
"Merry Christmas, my dear, but next year NO BIKE!"

P. R. Van Buskirk

Is There a Santa Claus?

(This famous editorial by Francis P. Church first appeared in The New York Sun, *September 21, 1897)*

We take pleasure in answering at once and thus prominently the communication below, expressing at the same time our great gratification that its faithful author is numbered among the friends of *The Sun:*

Dear Editor:

I am 8 years old.

Some of my little friends say there is no Santa Claus.

Papa says "If you see it in *The Sun* it's so."

Please tell me the truth, is there a Santa Claus?

Virginia O'Hanlon
115 West 95th Street

Virginia, your little friends are wrong. They have been affected by the skepticism of a skeptical age. They do not believe except what they see. They think that nothing can be which is not comprehensible by their little minds. All minds, Virginia, whether they be men's or children's, are little. In this great universe of ours man is a mere insect, an ant, in his intellect, as compared with the boundless world about him, as measured by the intelligence capable of grasping the whole of truth and knowledge.

Yes, Virginia, there is a Santa Claus. He exists as certainly as love and generosity and devotion exist, and you know that they abound and give to your life its highest beauty and joy. Alas! how dreary would be the world if there were no Santa Claus! It would be as dreary as if there were no Virginias. There would be no childlike faith then, no poetry, no romance to make tolerable this existence. We should have no enjoyment, except in sense and sight. The eternal light with which childhood fills the world would be extinguished.

Not believe in Santa Claus! You might as well not believe in fairies! You might get your papa to hire men to watch in all the chimneys on Christmas eve to catch Santa Claus, but even if they did not see Santa Claus coming down, what would that prove? Nobody sees Santa Claus, but that is no sign that there is no Santa Claus. The most real things in the world are those that neither children nor men can see. Did you ever see fairies dancing on the lawn? Of course not, but that's no proof that they are not there. Nobody can conceive or imagine all the wonders there are unseen and unseeable in the world.

You tear apart the baby's rattle and see what makes the noise inside, but there is a veil covering the unseen world which not the strongest man, nor even the united strength of all the strongest men that ever lived, could tear apart. Only faith, fancy, poetry, love, romance, can push aside that curtain and view and picture the supernal beauty and glory beyond. Is it all real? Ah, Virginia, in all this world there is nothing else real and abiding.

No Santa Claus! Thank God he lives, and he lives forever. A thousand years from now, Virginia, nay, ten times ten thousand years from now, he will continue to make glad the heart of childhood.

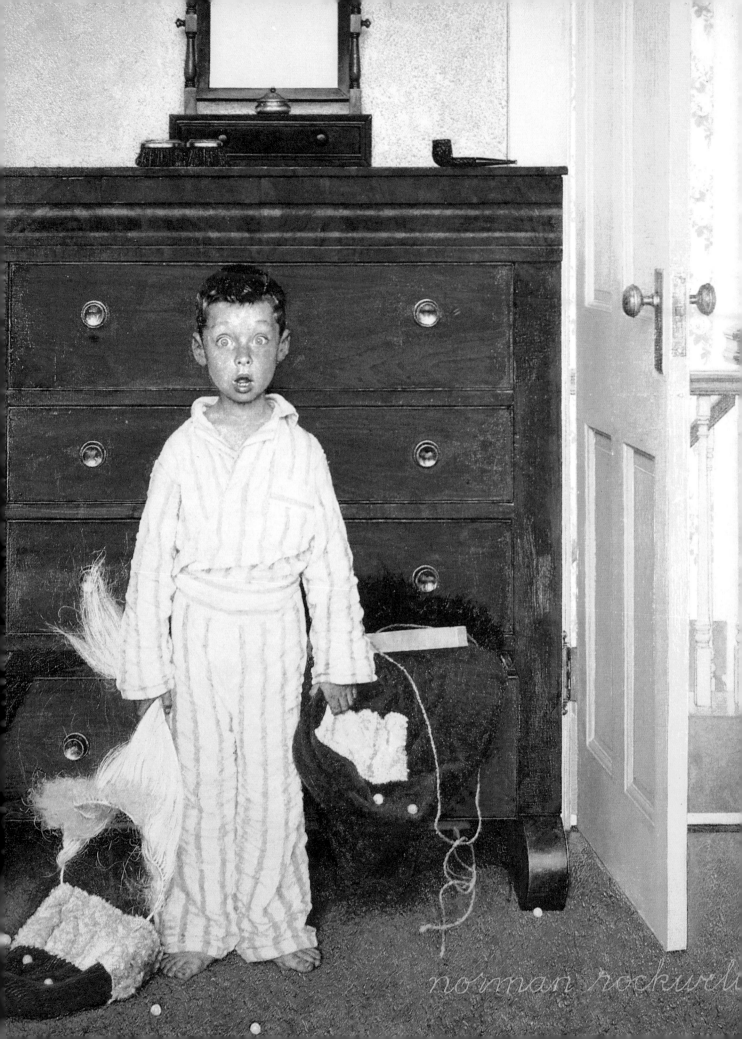

norman rockwell

Santa's Coming

The stars are frosty against the sky,
and the North Wind whistles shrill;
The snow is blowing against the house
and drifting across the hill.
And away up North, a reindeer team
is harnessed and eager for flight:
The sleigh is loaded with lovely toys,
for Santa Claus comes tonight!

And now he is ready. The little team
leaps into the northern sky
Lighter than any wind that blows —
Gracious! how fast they fly!
The gay, sweet bells on Santa's sleigh
play a merry tinkling tune,
And Santa laughs as his little team
wins a race with the Man-in-the-Moon.

Faster than ever they're coming now,
down the slippery milky way.
(They have to return to their home, you know,
ere the dawn of Christmas day.)

And Santa has many a mile to go
   and many a task to do,
For he must visit Bobby and Tom,
   and Carol and Jane and Sue —

Hush! I think I hear the sleigh bells,
   Hear the patter of a hoof;
Hear old Santa's cheery chuckle
   as he walks across our roof.
He'll come sliding down the chimney,
   for he doesn't mind the fire,
And in the pack upon his back
   he'll have your heart's desire —

Oh, eager restless little girl,
   now hurry into bed,
And draw the blankets tight
   and warm above your curly head.
Oh, close your eyes, you funny child —
   now don't you hear him creep?
Santa never visits little ones
   who aren't fast asleep!

       Mrs. Roy L. Peifer

Overleaf
FOREST FOLK CAROLS
Dennis Hockerman

We wish you a Merry Christmas
And a Happy New Year!

The Magic Tree

The forest folk live in a magic tree;
They celebrate Christmas for all to see:

White-bearded Santas in bowties and caps;
Wrinkled old gnomes just awake from their naps;
Men made of snow, with carrot stick noses,
Who wield hockey sticks in ridiculous poses;

Camels with bracelets and rings round their knees
And saddles with tassels and bells, if you please!
Reindeer in flight with antlers for wings
And backpacks for carrying presents and things;

At the base of the tree, mane flying askance,
Is a friendly beast, you can tell by a glance,
With tail twined around the trunk of the tree,
He lends it his weighty support, you see.

At the top of the tree, a sight to behold!
An elephant hovers with wings of gold;
The star is poised on his trunk upright
And its light shines forth on Christmas night.

The forest folk live in a magic tree;
They celebrate Christmas for all to see.

Cathy Reynolds

Overleaf
BALLOONS IN THE SNOW
John Warden

The Joy of Giving

Somehow, not only for Christmas
But all the long year through,
The joy that you give to others
Is the joy that comes back to you;
And the more you spend in blessing
The poor and lonely and sad,
The more of your heart's possessing
Returns to make you glad.

John Greenleaf Whittier

Magic of Christmas

There's a magic that comes with Christmas,
A magic that fills the heart,
And it glistens in every window
Of village, town, and mart.
There's a magic that comes with Christmas
In Santa and fairy trees,
In the laughter of merry children,
And people on bended knees.

There's a magic that comes with Christmas,
A magic for old and young,
For it seems that people are kinder
When simple carols are sung.
There's a magic that comes with Christmas,
As the scarlet candles glow,
Because Christ was born in a manger
In Bethlehem long ago.

Hilda Butler Farr

Post-Christmas Rhyme

Before the festive berries fall
    Like jeweled rain; before the tree
That stands in aromatic green
    Is stripped of shining finery;
Before the heart's high brimming cup
    Holds one drop less of fiery dew —
Pray God that all of us may keep
    One Christmas spark the whole year through.

Rachel Field

POST-CHRISTMAS RHYME by Rachel Field reprinted with permission of Macmillan Publishing Company from POEMS by Rachel Field. Copyright 1941 by Rachel Field Pederson, renewed 1969 by Arthur S. Pederson.

Mistletoe

Sitting under the mistletoe
(Pale-green, fairy mistletoe),
One last candle burning low,
All the sleepy dancers gone,
Just one candle burning on,
Shadows lurking everywhere:
Some one came, and kissed me there.

Tired I was; my head would go
Nodding under the mistletoe
(Pale-green, fairy mistletoe),
No footsteps came, no voice, but only
Just as I sat there, sleepy, lonely,
Stooped in the still and shadowy air
Lips unseen — and kissed me there.

Walter de la Mare

MISTLETOE by Walter de la Mare reprinted with permission of The Literary Trustees of Walter de la Mare and The Society of Authors as their representative.

Firwood

The fir trees taper into twigs and wear
The rich blue green of summer all the year,
Softening the roughest tempest almost calm
And offering shelter ever still and warm
To the small path that towels underneath,
Where loudest winds — almost as summer's breath —
Scarce fan the weed that lingers green below,
When others out of doors are lost in frost and snow.
And sweet the music trembles on the ear
As the wind suthers through each tiny spear,
Makeshifts for leaves; and yet, so rich they show,
Winter is almost summer where they grow.

John Clare

A Winter Ride

Who shall declare the joy of running!
　Who shall tell of the pleasures of flight!
Springing and spurning the tufts of wild heather,
　Sweeping, wide-winged, through the blue dome of light.
Everything mortal has moments immortal,
　Swift and God-gifted, immeasurably bright.
So with the stretch of the white road before me
　Shining snow crystals rainbowed by the sun,
Fields that are white, stained with long, cool, blue shadows,
　Strong with the strength of my horse as we run.
Joy in the touch of the wind and the sunlight!
　Joy! With the vigorous earth I am one.

Amy Lowell

The Bells

Hear the sledges with the bells,
    Silver bells!
What a world of merriment their melody foretells!
    How they tinkle, tinkle, tinkle,
      In the icy air of night!
While the stars that oversprinkle
All the heavens seem to twinkle
      With a crystalline delight;
    Keeping time, time, time,
    In a sort of Runic rhyme,
To the tintinabulation that so musically wells
    From the bells, bells, bells, bells,
      Bells, bells, bells —
    From the jingling and the tinkling of the bells.

Edgar Allan Poe

A Christmas Message

We celebrate this holiday season with special pleasure and pride here at Ideals; forty years ago this Christmas the first Ideals issue was published.

It was a time of sorrow and despair for many; World Warr II raged on, longer than anyone had imagined possible. The war effort exacted personal and economic sacrifices from Americans at home and abroad. In the midst of such troubled times, a man with a vision of hope for a better world launched Ideals magazine.

In the words of its founder, Van B. Hooper, "As the name implies, Ideals is a book of old fashioned ideals, homey philosophy, poetry, music, inspiration and art — things some of us may have overlooked during these busy days." The first Ideals issue was run as a limited edition because of the severe paper shortage during the war. It struck an immediately responsive chord with its readers and has continued to do so over the years.

In these relatively peaceful (although potentially volatile) and certainly busier-than-ever days, we trust that Ideals will continue to serve as a source of hope and inspiration to its readers.

All of us here at Ideals wish you a blessed Christmas and a peaceful New Year.

The Edito

ACKNOWLEDGMENTS

CHRISTMAS EVERYWHERE from CHRISTMAS SONGS AND EASTER BALLADS by P lips Brooks, copyright © 1903 by E. P. Dutton & Co., Inc. DECEMBER by Aileen Fis from THAT'S WHY, Thomas Nelson & Sons, New York, 1946. Copyright renewed 19 Reprinted by permission of author. Recipes for GINGERBREAD HOUSE by Carole Jar SANTA'S COMING by Mrs. Roy L. Peifer from REFLECTIONS OF CHRISTMAS, copyri 1955 by Wheelabrator Corp., Mishawaka, Indiana. COME, SING A HALE HEIGH-HO from THE CHRISTMAS LONG AGO in JOYFUL POEMS FOR CHILDREN by James W comb Riley. CHRISTMAS BELLS, THE CHRISTMAS HOLLY by Eliza Cook, A CHRISTMS CAROL by Josiah Gilbert Holland, and A CHRISTMAS LULLABY by John Addington monds from OUR AMERICAN HOLIDAYS, CHRISTMAS, edited by Robert Haven Sch ler. I AM THINKING OF YOU...from THE SPIRIT OF CHRISTMAS by Henry van Dy copyright 1905 by Charles Scribner's Sons. A CHRISTMAS WISH from GRACE WALKE SCRAPBOOK, copyright 1940 by Northland Publishing House.